Metal

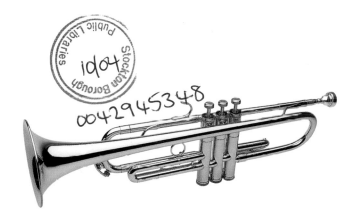

by Claire Llewellyn

W

FRANKLIN WATTS

LONDON • SYDNEY

First published in 2002 by
Franklin Watts
96 Leonard Street
London EC2A 4XD

Franklin Watts Australia
45-51 Huntley Street
Alexandria
NSW 2015

Text copyright © Claire Llewellyn 2002

ISBN 0 7496 3990 3

Dewey Decimal
Classification Number: 669

A CIP catalogue record for this book is
available from the British Library

Series editor: Rosalind Beckman
Series designer: James Evans
Picture research: Diana Morris
Photography: Steve Shott

Printed in Hong Kong, China

Acknowledgements

Thanks are due to the following for kind permission to
reproduce photographs:

AKG London: 7cl. Klaus Andrews/Still Pictures: 9t. Mark
Andrews/Still Pictures: 9c. Austrian Archives/Corbis: 16b. Yann
Arthus-Betrand/Corbis: 26c. Boodle & Dunthorne: 16cr. BSIP,
Boucharlat/SPL: 13t. John Cancalosi/Still Pictures: 18c. Christies
Images/Corbis: 20b. James Davis Travel Photography: 8b. Chris
Fairclough/Franklin Watts: 25b. Favre Felix/Jerrican/ SPL: 22b
Dylan Garcia/Still Pictures: 24b. Ron Giling/Still Pictures: 18b.
Gunshots/The Art Archive: 12t, 12b. Ben Johnson/SPL: 26b.
Damien Lovegrove/SPL: 27c. John Mead/SPL: 27t. Ray
Moller/Franklin Watts: 15t. Dagli Orti/Historical Museum
Sofia/The Art Archive: 16t. Vittoriano Rastelli/Corbis: 10b.
Rosenfeld Images Ltd/SPL: 23c. Charles E Rotkin/Corbis: b
cover. Horst Scafer/Still Pictures: 25t. Paul Seheult/Eye
Ubiquitous: 21t. Heine Schneebelj/SPL: 19t. Kaj R Svensson/
SPL: 18t. Hugh Turvey/SPL: 7br. Nick Wiseman/Eye
Ubiquitous: 17t. Dove Wren/Eye Ubiquitous: 23t.

Thanks are also due to John Lewis for their help
with this book.

Contents

Words printed in **bold italic** are explained in the glossary.

What is metal?

Metal is one of the world's most useful materials. Look around and you'll see that we use it everywhere - in our cars, offices, homes and schools. It is hard to imagine life without it.

All sorts of metals

There are over 80 different kinds of metal. One metal can look and feel a little different from another, and may be used in different ways.

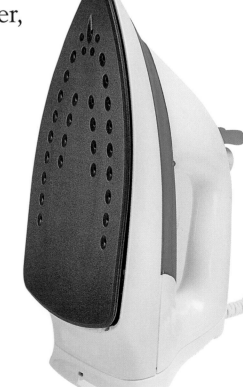

Made of metal

All the things in these pictures are made of metal. Can you name them all? What do they feel like when you touch them?

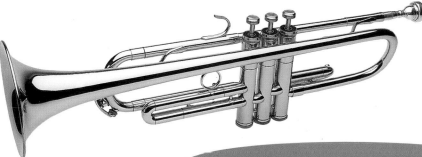

Material words

Which of these words describe metal?

cold   thick   shiny

sticky   stretchy

heavy   stiff   solid

dull   soft   strong

hard   warm

hard-wearing

spongy   light

crisp   colourful

rough   smooth

thin

bendy   slimy

springy

runny   squashy

Fantastic fact

Most metals are solid, but one is liquid. It is called mercury and is used in thermometers.

Metal is hard and strong

Many metals are hard and strong, and can stand up to very heavy wear. That is why metal is used to make buildings, machines and cars.

Standing strong

Most big buildings have a framework inside them made of metal beams. The metal framework holds up the building and stops it falling down. Many bridges hang from metal cables or are made from metal beams.

The Golden Gate bridge in San Francisco hangs from strong metal cables that run down into the ground.

Working hard

Think of all the machines that are made of metal - washing machines, factory machines, cars, drills, cranes and so on. All these machines have moving parts. Metal is the only material that could take such wear and tear.

Factory and farming machines need to be strong because they are used for heavy work. They are mostly made of metal.

Try this

watercress

Eat a little spinach or watercress and you are eating a metal called iron. Many foods contain tiny bits of metal. They are very good for the body and help to keep you strong.

spinach

Metal is smooth and shiny

Most metal is smooth and easy to clean, and often looks very shiny. But if you do not clean them, some metals lose their shine. They grow dull or even *rusty*.

Keeping clean

Large kitchens, where hundreds of meals are cooked every day, have lots of metal equipment. This is because it is hard-wearing and easy to keep clean. At home, kitchen sinks and taps are often made of metal, too.

Restaurant kitchens need to be free of germs. Metal tools and worktops are easy to clean.

Staying shiny

Silver cutlery and candlesticks look beautiful when they are polished. But after a while the metal goes dull and needs cleaning again. Some metals need extra care if they are out of doors because the damp air makes them go rusty.

Silver candlesticks only stay shiny if they are cleaned regularly.

These garden shears are going rusty. They need to be cleaned and oiled.

Try this

Find a dirty metal object such as an old spoon or coin, and polish it with a cloth and some metal cleaner. What happens to the object? What happens to the cloth?

Metal can be very sharp

Metal is so hard that if you rub it with a stone, it will become very sharp. Metal has been used to make tools and weapons for many thousands of years.

Metal weapons

When people discovered metal about 8,000 years ago, they used it to make weapons. Metal spearheads, swords and axes were sharp and strong. They were better for hunting and fighting than weapons made of wood or stone.

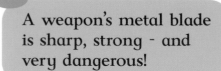

A weapon's metal blade is sharp, strong - and very dangerous!

Metal tools

Many tools have a sharp metal blade. They are used to cut other materials. Saws, axes, scissors and knives are part of our everyday lives. They are used in hospitals, restaurants, forests and farms.

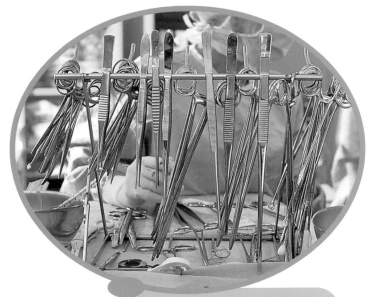

Sharp metal tools are used by doctors in the operating theatre.

WARNING

Always take care with sharp tools. They can easily cut you.

Try this

Find two trowels – one made of metal, the other made of plastic. Try digging with them both. Is there any difference between them?

Metal carries heat and electricity

Materials that allow heat or **electricity** to pass through them are called **conductors**. Metal is a very useful material because it conducts both heat and electricity.

Carrying heat

Metal allows heat to pass through it quickly. If you put a metal saucepan over a flame, it heats up and starts to cook the food. Many hot machines such as ovens and irons are also made of metal.

Cakes bake best on a hot, metal tray.

Most metal saucepans have a wooden or plastic handle. A metal handle would heat up very quickly and be uncomfortable to hold.

Carrying electricity

Electricity is carried along metal wires from power stations to our homes. Electricity can be dangerous, so the wires are wrapped inside plastic flex. Plastic does not conduct electricity, so this keeps the electricity out of reach.

Plastic flex makes electric things safe to use.

Inside a light bulb is a thin metal thread. When electricity flows across the metal, the thread glows and gives out light.

This piece of plastic flex has been cut away to show the metal wires inside.

Try this

Take two metal teaspoons. Put one in a mug of cold water and the other in a mug of hot water. Leave them to stand for a few minutes. Now take them out, dry them and feel them. What do you notice?

Some metals are precious

Some metals such as gold, silver and *platinum* are not easily found. They are called precious metals and are used to make special things.

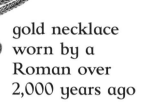

gold necklace worn by a Roman over 2,000 years ago

Rare metals

gold and cameo bracelet

Some metals such as iron are very common and used to make many things. Other metals are more rare. Gold and platinum are the most precious metals. They have a beautiful colour and shine.

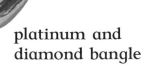

platinum and diamond bangle

white gold and diamond necklace

gold earrings

Precious goods

People have always prized precious metals and used them to make *jewellery* and other beautiful things. Gold and silver were used to make the first coins because they showed the value of the money. Today's coins are made from much cheaper metals.

Churches are special buildings. The roof of this Russian church has been covered with gold to make it look important.

These coins are about 500 years old. Can you see when the largest one was made?

Fantastic fact

The front of an astronaut's helmet has a fine coating of gold. When bright sunlight hits the gold, it bounces back off again. This protects the astronaut's eyes from being damaged by the Sun.

Metal is dug out of the ground

A few metals are found in lumps called **nuggets**, but most are found inside rocks. The rocks have to be dug up and heated before the metal can be used.

Nuggets of gold (left) and copper (top). Only gold, silver, platinum and copper are found as nuggets.

Digging up ores

Most metals are hidden inside rocks called **ores** and have to be dug out of the ground. This is sometimes done in open **quarries**, but more often in underground mines. Mining is hard, dirty and dangerous work and can cost human lives.

This worker is mining for copper. His powerful drill is able to reach the metal ore deep inside the rock.

It takes the heat of a huge furnace to get the metal out of an ore.

Treating the ores

To get the metal out of the rock, the ore must be crushed and heated in a *furnace*. The metal then melts and can be poured away. As it cools, it turns hard again and can be used to make many things.

Fantastic fact

The deepest mine in the world is a gold mine in South Africa. The miners have to work 4 km under the ground.

Metals can be mixed together

Metals can often be made better or stronger by mixing two of them together. The new mixture is called an **alloy**.

From copper to bronze

Copper was one of the first metals ever to be used. It was quite soft and easy to hammer. In time, people discovered that if they heated the copper and mixed it with a metal called tin, they produced a much harder metal that could be used to make weapons and tools. The new metal was called bronze.

Copper is a reddish-brown metal. Today, we use it to make the wires that carry electricity. It also makes the best pots and pans.

Since ancient times bronze has been used to make statues and sculptures such as this African mask.

Stainless steel

Steel is a very strong metal made from iron. But steel will rust in the open air. When it is mixed with other metals, it produces an alloy called *stainless steel*. Stainless steel is very useful. It is used to make many things because it is strong and does not rust.

Kitchen tools are often made of stainless steel. They do not rust, even though they are always getting wet.

Try this

Find some nails made of iron or steel. Put a few in a dry jar and a few in a jar half-filled with water. Seal both jars with a lid. Leave the jars for two weeks, then examine the nails. What do you find?

Metal is easy to shape

If metal is heated until it softens or melts, it can be shaped into many different goods. This is usually done by factory machines.

Into a mould

Metal melts when it is heated and hardens when it cools. While it is soft, it can be shaped in a number of different ways. It can be poured into a **mould** and left to cool until it sets into a solid shape.

Red-hot metal is poured into a mould. It is being used to make a bell.

Pressing and squeezing

Hot metal can be flattened by heavy rollers to make beams, sheets and rails. It can be squeezed through small holes to make thin rods or wire. It can also be pressed into different shapes, such as the doors or boot of a car.

A blacksmith hammers softened metal into the shape of a horseshoe.

Metal can be rolled into long flat sheets of many different thicknesses.

Fantastic fact

Thin sheets of *aluminium* foil are used to wrap up food. Aluminium is one of the few metals that can be crushed into a ball!

Metal can be recycled

When people buy new metal goods, they throw the old ones away. This is a waste. The metal can be **recycled** and used to make new things. This protects our **environment**.

Why recycle?

Getting rid of old metal goods can be a problem. Metal does not burn or rot away easily. The best thing is to recycle it. Recycling metal saves the **energy** that is used to dig up, crush and heat the ores. This cuts down the **pollution** that comes from burning fuels.

Old, rusting metal goods can be sharp and dangerous.

When these old cars have been melted down, the metal will be used to make many other things.

From scrap to steel

Old metal goods such as fridges and cars can be taken to a scrapyard. The steel they contain is melted down and used to make new things. Recycling saves the material itself and the energy that was used to make it.

Fantastic fact

A baked bean tin may contain steel that was once part of a car. When the can is next recycled, it might end up in a ship or a razor blade.

New cans from old

Drinks cans are made from aluminium. Aluminium is expensive to produce and causes damage to the environment. Never throw away an aluminium can because it can easily be recycled.

What is aluminium?

Aluminium is a very light metal that is used to make many things. It is produced from an ore called *bauxite*. Bauxite is found in hot places such as rainforests.
The bauxite is taken to a factory, where it is heated to produce aluminium.

Huge areas of rainforest are cut down in order to dig up the bauxite.

Lumps of bauxite need to be heated to very high temperatures to produce aluminium. This takes a lot of energy.

Recycling aluminium

Aluminium is used to make drinks cans, which can be recycled when they are empty. The cans are collected in can banks and crushed into **bales**.

Empty aluminium cans are collected in canbanks.

At the recycling factory, the bales are heated until they melt. As the aluminium cools and begins to harden, it is rolled into new metal sheets.

This bale of crushed cans will be recycled into brand new cans.

Try this

Aluminium cans look the same as cans made of steel. Sort one from the other by using a magnet. What happens when you put the magnet near an aluminium can? What happens when you put it near a steel one?

Glossary

Alloy	A metal that is made by mixing two or more metals together.
Aluminium	A light, silver-coloured metal that is used to make drinks cans and many other things.
Bale	A large bundle.
Bauxite	An ore than contains aluminium.
Conductor	A material such as metal that allows heat or electricity to pass through it easily.
Copper	A soft, reddish-brown metal.
Electricity	A kind of energy that provides us with heat, light and the power for machines.
Energy	The power that makes machines and living things able to work.
Environment	The world around us, including the land, the air and the sea.
Furnace	A very hot oven.
Jewellery	Things like bracelets, necklaces and rings that are worn for decoration.

Mould	A container with a special shape. Melted metal can be poured into a mould to take on its shape.
Nugget	A lump of gold or other metal.
Ore	A rock that contains metal.
Platinum	A silvery-white precious metal.
Pollution	Spoiling the air, land or water with harmful substances.
Quarry	A place where rocks are dug out of the ground.
Recycle	To take an object or material and use it to make something else.
Rust	A reddish-brown coating that forms on some metals when they are left in the damp.
Stainless steel	An alloy that does not rust and is used to make cutlery and many other things.
Steel	A very strong alloy that is made from iron and is used in buildings and machines.

Index